The country justice. A poem. By one of His Majesty's Justices of the Peace for the county of Somerset. Part the first.

John Langhorne

ECCO
PRINT EDITIONS

Eighteenth Century
Collections Online
Print Editions

Gale ECCO Print Editions

Relive history with *Eighteenth Century Collections Online*, now available in print for the independent historian and collector. This series includes the most significant English-language and foreign-language works printed in Great Britain during the eighteenth century, and is organized in seven different subject areas including literature and language; medicine, science, and technology; and religion and philosophy. The collection also includes thousands of important works from the Americas.

The eighteenth century has been called "The Age of Enlightenment." It was a period of rapid advance in print culture and publishing, in world exploration, and in the rapid growth of science and technology – all of which had a profound impact on the political and cultural landscape. At the end of the century the American Revolution, French Revolution and Industrial Revolution, perhaps three of the most significant events in modern history, set in motion developments that eventually dominated world political, economic, and social life.

In a groundbreaking effort, Gale initiated a revolution of its own: digitization of epic proportions to preserve these invaluable works in the largest online archive of its kind. Contributions from major world libraries constitute over 175,000 original printed works. Scanned images of the actual pages, rather than transcriptions, recreate the works ***as they first appeared.***

Now for the first time, these high-quality digital scans of original works are available via print-on-demand, making them readily accessible to libraries, students, independent scholars, and readers of all ages.

For our initial release we have created seven robust collections to form one the world's most comprehensive catalogs of 18th century works.

Initial Gale ECCO Print Editions collections include:

History and Geography
Rich in titles on English life and social history, this collection spans the world as it was known to eighteenth-century historians and explorers. Titles include a wealth of travel accounts and diaries, histories of nations from throughout the world, and maps and charts of a world that was still being discovered. Students of the War of American Independence will find fascinating accounts from the British side of conflict.

Social Science

Delve into what it was like to live during the eighteenth century by reading the first-hand accounts of everyday people, including city dwellers and farmers, businessmen and bankers, artisans and merchants, artists and their patrons, politicians and their constituents. Original texts make the American, French, and Industrial revolutions vividly contemporary.

Medicine, Science and Technology

Medical theory and practice of the 1700s developed rapidly, as is evidenced by the extensive collection, which includes descriptions of diseases, their conditions, and treatments. Books on science and technology, agriculture, military technology, natural philosophy, even cookbooks, are all contained here.

Literature and Language

Western literary study flows out of eighteenth-century works by Alexander Pope, Daniel Defoe, Henry Fielding, Frances Burney, Denis Diderot, Johann Gottfried Herder, Johann Wolfgang von Goethe, and others. Experience the birth of the modern novel, or compare the development of language using dictionaries and grammar discourses.

Religion and Philosophy

The Age of Enlightenment profoundly enriched religious and philosophical understanding and continues to influence present-day thinking. Works collected here include masterpieces by David Hume, Immanuel Kant, and Jean-Jacques Rousseau, as well as religious sermons and moral debates on the issues of the day, such as the slave trade. The Age of Reason saw conflict between Protestantism and Catholicism transformed into one between faith and logic -- a debate that continues in the twenty-first century.

Law and Reference

This collection reveals the history of English common law and Empire law in a vastly changing world of British expansion. Dominating the legal field is the *Commentaries of the Law of England* by Sir William Blackstone, which first appeared in 1765. Reference works such as almanacs and catalogues continue to educate us by revealing the day-to-day workings of society.

Fine Arts

The eighteenth-century fascination with Greek and Roman antiquity followed the systematic excavation of the ruins at Pompeii and Herculaneum in southern Italy; and after 1750 a neoclassical style dominated all artistic fields. The titles here trace developments in mostly English-language works on painting, sculpture, architecture, music, theater, and other disciplines. Instructional works on musical instruments, catalogs of art objects, comic operas, and more are also included.

The BiblioLife Network

This project was made possible in part by the BiblioLife Network (BLN), a project aimed at addressing some of the huge challenges facing book preservationists around the world. The BLN includes libraries, library networks, archives, subject matter experts, online communities and library service providers. We believe every book ever published should be available as a high-quality print reproduction; printed on-demand anywhere in the world. This insures the ongoing accessibility of the content and helps generate sustainable revenue for the libraries and organizations that work to preserve these important materials.

The following book is in the "public domain" and represents an authentic reproduction of the text as printed by the original publisher. While we have attempted to accurately maintain the integrity of the original work, there are sometimes problems with the original work or the micro-film from which the books were digitized. This can result in minor errors in reproduction. Possible imperfections include missing and blurred pages, poor pictures, markings and other reproduction issues beyond our control. Because this work is culturally important, we have made it available as part of our commitment to protecting, preserving, and promoting the world's literature.

GUIDE TO FOLD-OUTS MAPS and OVERSIZED IMAGES

The book you are reading was digitized from microfilm captured over the past thirty to forty years. Years after the creation of the original microfilm, the book was converted to digital files and made available in an online database.

In an online database, page images do not need to conform to the size restrictions found in a printed book. When converting these images back into a printed bound book, the page sizes are standardized in ways that maintain the detail of the original. For large images, such as fold-out maps, the original page image is split into two or more pages

Guidelines used to determine how to split the page image follows:

• Some images are split vertically; large images require vertical and horizontal splits.
• For horizontal splits, the content is split left to right.
• For vertical splits, the content is split from top to bottom.
• For both vertical and horizontal splits, the image is processed from top left to bottom right.

THE

COUNTRY JUSTICE.

A POEM.

BY ONE OF HIS MAJESTY's JUSTICES OF THE

PEACE FOR THE COUNTY OF SOMERSET.

PART THE FIRST.

LONDON.

Printed for T. BECKET, the Corner of the ADELPHI,

in the Strand. MDCCLXXIV.

RICHARD BURN, LL. D.

ONE OF HIS MAJESTY's JUSTICES OF THE PEACE
FOR THE COUNTIES OF WESTMORLAND
AND CUMBERLAND.

DEAR SIR,

A POEM written profeſſedly at your requeſt, naturally addreſſes itſelf to you. The diſtinction you have acquired on the ſubject, and your taſte for the arts, give that addreſs every kind of propriety. If I have any particular ſatisfaction in this publication, beſide what ariſes from my

B   compliance

compliance with your commands, it muſt be in the idea of that teſtimony it bears to our Friendſhip. If you believe that I am more concerned for the duration of that than of the Poem itſelf, you will not be miſtaken; for I am,

Dear Sir,

Your truly affectionate Brother,

and faithful humble Servant,

Somerſetſhire,
April 25, 1774.

THE AUTHOR.

THE

COUNTRY JUSTICE.

INTRODUCTION.

IN RICHARD's days, when loft his paftured plain,

    The wand'ring Briton fought the wild wood's reign,

With great difdain beheld the feudal Hord,

Poor life-lett Vaffals of a Norman Lord ;

And, what no brave man ever loft, poffefs'd

Himfelf,——for Freedom bound him to her Breaft.

    Lov'ft Thou that Freedom ? By her holy fhrine,

If yet one drop of Britifh Blood be thine,

See

See, I conjure Thee, in the defart fhade,

His Bow unftrung, his little houfehold laid,

Some brave Forefather; while his Fields they fhare,

By Saxon, Dane, or Norman banifh'd there!

And think He tells Thee, as his Soul withdraws,

As his Heart fwells againft a Tyrant's Laws,

The War with Fate though fruitlefs to maintain,

To guard that Liberty he lov'd in vain.

Were thoughts like thefe the Dream of ancient
    Time?

Peculiar only to fome Age, or Clime?

And does not Nature thoughts like thefe impart,

Breathe in the Soul, and write upon the Heart?

Afk on their Mountains yon deferted Band,

That point to PAOLI with no plaufive Hand,

Defpifing ftill, their freeborn Souls unbroke,

Alike the *Gallic* and *Ligurian* Yoke!

                                    Yet

Yet while the Patriots' gen'rous rage we fhare,

Still *civil Safety* calls us back to Care ;—

To Britain loft in either HENRY's day,

Her Woods, her Mountains one wild Scene of Prey !

Fair Peace from all her bounteous Vallies fled,

And Law beneath the barbed Arrow bled.

In happier Days, with more aufpicious Fate,

The far-fam'd Edward heal'd his wounded State ;

Dread of his Foes, but to his Subjects dear,

Thefe learn'd to love, as thofe are taught to fear,

Their laurell'd Prince with Britifh Pride obey,

His Glory fhone their Difcontent away.

With Care the tender Flow'r of Love to fave,

And plant the Olive on *Diforder*'s Grave,

For civil Storms frefh Barriers to provide,

He caught the fav'ring Calm and falling Tide.

C

The

The Appointment, and its Purposes.

The social Laws from Insult to protect,

To cherish Peace, to cultivate Respect ;

The rich from wanton Cruelty restrain,

To smooth the Bed of Penury and Pain ;

The hapless Vagrant to his Rest restore,

The maze of Fraud, the Haunts of Theft explore ;

The thoughtless Maiden, when subdu'd by Art,

To aid, and bring her Rover to her Heart ;

Wild Riot's Voice with Dignity to quell,

Forbid unpeaceful Passions to rebel,

Wrest from Revenge the meditated Harm,

For this fair JUSTICE raised her sacred Arm ;

For this the rural Magistrate, of Yore,

Thy Honours, Edward, to his Mansion bore.

Antient

Antient Justice's Hall.

Oft, where old Air in conscious Glory sails,

On silver Waves that flow thro' smiling Vales.

In Harewood's Groves, where long my Youth was laid,

Unseen beneath their antient World of Shade,

With many a Group of antique Columns crown'd,

In Gothic Guise such Mansion have I found.

Nor lightly deem, ye Apes of modern Race,

Ye Cits that sore bedizen Nature's Face,

Of the more manly Structures here ye view ;

They rose for Greatness that ye never knew !

Ye reptile Cits, that oft have mov'd my Spleen

With Venus, and the Graces on your Green !

Let Plutus, growling o'er his ill-got Wealth,

Let Mercury, the thriving God of Stealth,

The Shopman, Janus, with his double Looks,

Rise on your Mounts, and perch upon your Books !

But,

But, fpare my Venus, fpare each Sifter Grace,

Ye Cits, that fore bedizen Nature's Face!

Ye royal Architects, whofe antic Tafte,

Would lay the Realms of Senfe and Nature wafte;

Forgot, whenever from her Steps ye ftray,

That Folly only points each other way;

Here, tho' your Eye no *courtly* Creature fees,

Snakes on the ground, or *Monkies* in the Trees;

Yet let not too fevere a Cenfure fall,

On the plain Precincts of the antient Hall.

For tho' no Sight your childifh Fancy meets,

Of Thibets' Dogs, or China's Perroquets;

Tho' Apes, Afps, Lizards, Things without a Tail,

And all the Tribes of foreign Monfters fail;

Here fhall ye figh to fee, with Ruft o'ergrown,

The Iron Griffin and the Sphynx of Stone;

And

And mourn, neglected in their wafte abodes,

Fire-breathing Drakes, and water-fpouting Gods.

Long have thefe mighty Monfters known Difgrace,

Yet ftill fome Trophies hold their ancient place;

Where, round the Hall, the Oak's high furbafe rears

The Field-day Triumphs of two hundred years.

Th' enormous Antlers here recal the day

That faw the Foreft-Monarch *forc'd away*;

Who, many a Flood, and many a Mountain paft,

Nor finding thofe, nor deeming thefe the laft,

O'er Floods, o'er Mountains yet prepar'd to fly,

Long ere the Death-drop fill'd his failing Eye!

Here, fam'd for Cunning, and in Crimes grown
  old,

Hangs his grey Brufh, the Felon of the Fold.

Oft, as the Rent Feaft fwells the Midnight Cheer,

The Maudlin Farmer kens him o'er his Beer,

And tells his old, traditionary Tale,

Tho' known to ev'ry Tenant of the Vale.

Here, where, of old, the feftal Ox has fed,

Mark'd with his weight, the mighty Horns are fpread:

Some Ox, O MARSHALL, for a Board like thine,

Where the vaft Mafter with the vaft Sir Loin

Vied in round Magnitude—Refpect I bear

To Thee, tho' oft the Ruin of the Chair.

Thefe, and fuch antique Tokens, that record

The manly Spirit, and the bounteous Board,

Me more delight than all the Gew-gaw Train,

The Whims and Zigzags of a modern Brain,

More than all Afia's Marmofets to view

Grin, frifk, and water in the Walks of Kew.

Character

Character of a Country Juſtice.

Thro' theſe fair Vallies, Stranger, haſt Thou ſtray'd,

By any Chance, to viſit HAREWOOD's Shade,

And ſeen with honeſt, antiquated Air,

In the plain Hall the Magiſtratial Chair ?

There HERBERT ſate—The Love of human kind,

Pure Light of Truth, and Temperance of Mind,

In the free Eye the featur'd Soul diſplay'd,

HONOUR's ſtrong Beam, and MERCY's melting Shade ;

JUSTICE, that, in the rigid Paths of Law,

Would ſtill ſome Drops from PITY's Fountain draw,

Bend o'er her Urn with many a gen'rous Fear,

Ere his firm Seal ſhould force one Orphan's Tear ;

Fair EQUITY, and REASON ſcorning Art,

And all the ſober Virtues of the Heart,——

Theſe

Thefe fate with HERBERT, thefe fhall beft avail,

Where Statutes order ; or where Statutes fail.

General Motives for Lenity.

Be this, ye rural Magiftrates, your Plan :

Firm be your Juftice, but be Friends to Man.

He whom the mighty Mafter of this Ball,

We fondly deem, or farcically call,

To own the Patriarch's Truth however loth,

Holds but a Manfion *crufh'd before the Moth.*

Frail in his Genius, in his Heart, too, frail,

Born but to err, and erring to bewail,

Shalt Thou his Faults with Eye fevere explore,

And give to Life one human Weaknefs more ?

Still mark if Vice or Nature prompts the Deed ;

Still mark the ftrong Temptation and the Need :

On

On preffing Want, on Famine's powerful call,
At leaft more lenient let thy Juftice fall.

Apology for Vagrants.

For Him, who, loft to ev'ry Hope of Life,

Has long with Fortune held unequal ftrife,

Known to no human Love, no human Care,

The friendlefs, homelefs Object of Defpair;

For the poor Vagrant, feel, while He complains,

Nor from fad Freedom fend to fadder Chains.

Alike, if Folly or Misfortune brought

Thofe laft of Woes his evil Days have wrought;

Believe with focial Mercy and with Me,

Folly's Misfortune in the firft Degree.

Perhaps on fome inhofpitable Shore

The houfelefs Wretch a widow d Parent bore,

Who, then, no more by golden Profpects led,

Of the poor Indian begg'd a Leafy bed.

E

Cold

Cold on Canadian Hills, or Minden's Plain,

Perhaps that Parent mourn'd her Soldier flain;

Bent o'er her Babe, her Eye diffolv'd in Dew,

The big Drops mingling with the Milk He drew,

Gave the fad Prefage of his future Years,

The Child of Mifery, baptiz'd in Tears!

Apoftrophe to EDWARD *the Third.*

O Edward, here thy faireft Laurels fade!

And thy long Glories darken into Shade!

While yet the Palms thy hardy Veterans won,

The Deeds of Valour that for thee were done,

While yet the Wreaths for which they bravely bled,

Fir'd thy high Soul, and flourifh'd on thy Head,

Thofe Veterans to their native Shores return'd,

Like Exiles wander'd, and like Exiles mourn'd;

Or,

Or, left *at large* no longer to bewail,

Were Vagrants deem'd, and deſtined to a jail!

  Were there no Royal, yet uncultur'd Lands,

No Waſtes that wanted ſuch ſubduing Hands?

Were CRESSY's Heroes ſuch abandon'd Things?

O Fate of War! and Gratitude of Kings!

       The Gypſey-Life.

  The Gypſey-Race my Pity rarely move;

Yet their ſtrong thirſt of Liberty I love.

Not WILKES, our Freedom's holy Martyr, more;

Nor his firm *Phalanx*, of the common Shore.

  For this in Norwood's patrimonial Groves,

The tawny Father with his Offspring roves;

When

When Summer Suns lead flow the fultry Day,

In moffy Caves, where welling Waters play,

Fann'd by each Gale that cools the fervid Sky,

With this in ragged Luxury they lie.

Oft at the Sun the dufky Elfins ftrain

The fable Eye, then, fnugging, fleep again;

Oft, as the Dews of cooler Evening fall,

For their prophetic Mother's Mantle call.

   Far other Cares that wandering Mother wait,

The Mouth, and oft the Minifter of Fate!

From her to hear, in Ev'ning's friendly fhade,

Of future Fortune, flies the Village-Maid,

Draws her long-hoarded Copper from its hold;

And rufty Halfpence purchafe hopes of Gold.

   But, ah! ye Maids, beware the Gypfey's Lures!

She opens not the Womb of Time, but yours.

Oft

Oft has her Hands the haplefs Marian wrung,

Marian, whom Gay in fweeteft Strains has fung!

The Parfon's Maid—fore Caufe had fhe to rue

The Gypfey's Tongue; the Parfon's Daughter too.

Long had that anxious Daughter figh'd to know

What Vellum's fprucy Clerk, the Valley's Beau,

Meant by thofe Glances, which at Church he ftole,

Her Father nodding to the Pfalm's flow Drawl;

Long had fhe figh'd, at length a Prophet came,

By many a fure Prediction known to Fame,

To Marian known, and all fhe told, for true :

She knew the future, for the paft fhe knew.

Where, in the darkling Shed, the Moon's dim Rays

Beam'd on the Ruins of a One-Horfe Chaife,

Villaria fate, while faithful Marian brought

The wayward Prophet of the Woe fhe fought.

F   Twice

Twice did her Hands, the Income of the Week,

On either side, the crooked Sixpence seek;

Twice were thofe Hands withdrawn from either side,

To flop the titt'ring Laugh, the Blufh to hide.

The wayward Prophet made no long Delay,

No Novice fhe in Fortune's devious way!

" Ere yet, fhe cried, ten rolling Months are o'er,

" Muft ye be Mothers, Maids, at leaft, no more.

" With you fhall foon, O Lady fair, prevail

" A gentle Youth, the Flower of this fair Vale.

" To MARIAN, once of Colin Clout the Scorn,

" Shall Bumkin come, and Bumkinets be born."

Smote to the Heart, the Maidens marvell'd fore,

That Ten fhort Months had fuch Events in ftore;

But holding firm, what Village-Maids believe,

That Strife with Fate is milking in a Sieve;

To

To prove their Prophet true, tho' to their Coft,

They juftly thought no Time was to be loft.

Thefe Foes to Youth, that feek, with dang'rous Art,

To aid the native Weaknefs of the Heart ;

Thefe Mifcreants from thy harmlefs Village drive,

As Wafps felonious from the lab'ring Hive.

END OF THE FIRST PART.

CPSIA information can be obtained at www.ICGtesting.com
Printed in the USA
LVOW10s2328030215

425518LV00014B/427/P